NAVIGATING TEENAGE REBELLION

NAVIGATING TEENAGE REBELLION

A Guide for Parents and Teachers

AVERY NIGHTINGALE

Creative Quill Press

CONTENTS

CHAPTER 1

Introduction

At one point or another, everyone has been a teenager; they have all experienced such feelings - frustration, oppression, and a sense of not being understood by both parents and especially by those in authority. Many teens have rebelled in one form or another, whether it be by standing up for what they believe, doing something their way and not someone else's, or going against an age-old custom or tradition. This rebellion, if handled constructively, can actually be a beneficial and necessary step in a teenager's development. At its best, rebellion can be a protest against a wrong or a way to test a new set of possibilities. At its worst, it can be destruction for its own sake and a way to reject that which is good, just because it comes from an authority figure. It is in dealing with the latter that parents often find themselves lost in a sea of confusion.

Every generation seems to have its own language it uses to confound or annoy older generations. The current phrase used by most teens when referring to their parents is "you just don't understand." This phrase is usually delivered with a heavy sigh and a roll of the eyes. Most adults do understand, or at least remember, what it was like to be a conscientious or even rebellious teenager. However, understanding and dealing with teenage rebellion is a different story. Ways of thinking have changed. The "generation gap" is a cliché, but it is indeed a truism that the chasm between parents and their teenage children is often a gaping one. This guide is intended to help parents effectively handle and survive this difficult time with their offspring.

CHAPTER 2

Understanding Teenage Rebellion

Adolescence is a time to break free from the family in preparation for establishing oneself in some form of social and economic independence. It is a time to weaken those psychological ties that have overly connected the person to the parents. While rebellion is often seen as dangerous "acting out" or rejecting all that the parents stand for, it is better viewed as a strategy to hasten separation. A strategy that usually features a conscious or unconscious dis-identification from parental values and behaviors, experimentation with different ways of living in the hope of stumbling upon something that works for the person. At best, the parents will encourage rebellion and be secure enough to tolerate some deviations from behaviors that they can endorse, but to varying degrees, the sight of their son or daughter doing something that they consider unwise or dangerous will unleash anxiety and anger as they attempt to reassert control.

This is a time of life when the young person is asking "Who am I?" One wants to develop an identity with a self-chosen occupation, morality, politics, religion, and peer group. One no longer wants an identity assigned according to the perceptions of parents and teachers. The young person wants to try out different roles, behaviors, and ideologies in an endless search for an identity that feels right. Often, this involves a painful and protracted separation from the parents and requires parents who have done the same thing and are secure in their own identity.

Development and the search for identity – who are you?

CHAPTER 3

Signs of Teenage Rebellion

Breaking the law/poor school performance. Obviously, illegal activity is unacceptable, but don't expect your rebellious child to obey this easily. You may have to get creative with punishments, keeping more of your child's free time consumed with constructive activities. Take away the TV and video games until his/her grades become satisfactory. With a little luck, this could even begin to quash some of the rebellion.

Change in friends. Let's face it, we all grow tired of our friends at some point. They may not be making the best decisions about how to spend their free time. Allowing your rebellious teenager to have too much freedom, especially if they've had to earn that privilege from you, is counter-productive to your goal to help him/her straighten out their life. Deciding with your teen which friends may not be best may seem impossible, and it may be. You can restrict your child from associating with a certain someone, but this usually provides more motivation for the unsupervised friendship. A more drastic measure might be sending your child to a school out-of-district. This decision can have lasting effects, and for better or worse, could be the wakeup call he/she needs. High school drop-outs soon question that decision, and a change of scenery may be best.

The blues. If your pre-teen or teenager is having persistent sadness, anxiety, lack of motivation, irritability, he or she may have a problem needing attention, not simply a bad attitude.

If you're worrying about your teenager's moodiness or rebelliousness, the answer may be right there in the mirror. However, striving for independence is healthy. Here are the signs, what's normal and what's not, and how to help your child navigate the teenage years.

CHAPTER 4

Causes of Teenage Rebellion

A better understanding of this can avert overreaction from parents who can see that all these actions are part of normal adolescent behavior.

Social causes are much different in the respect that they are sought out by the adolescent and can actually be seen as a positive experience despite the potential negative consequences. Examples of this are experimenting with drugs or alcohol, the formation of a new peer group, or the decision to date someone who is deemed unsuitable by the adolescent's parents. These situations all carry potential negative outcomes, but it is often noted by adults that punishment for these actions only causes the child to rebel further. This is due to the fact that the child does not perceive these actions as bad, but rather as ways to achieve grown-up status and privileges.

Distinguish between social and societal causes. This is an inexact science, but generally speaking, societal causes for teenage rebellion will be those events forced upon the adolescent, and social causes are those that the teen seeks out on their own. Societal causes could include the divorce of the adolescent's parents, moving to a new town, or changing schools. These are events that will affect the teen whether they like it or not and will often cause increased levels of stress while the teen is forced to adapt to the new situation.

CHAPTER 5

Impact of Teenage Rebellion on Adolescents

The result of even more minor acts of rebellion can create further distance between the parent and the teenager. This includes an increase in secretive behavior and contemplation of running away from home. Although the act of running away is a very small percentage of the said behaviors, it is an ultimate statement of separation and individuation and usually is the climax of a series of acts of rebellion. Often times, it is this form of rebellion that has the greatest impact on the teenager and can be a cause of harmful effects on the adolescent. This is not to say that the act of running away is harmful, but rather the events and feelings leading up to that decision.

Teenage rebellion is defined as "the movement of the adolescent away from the wishes of the parents as a means of individuating." This can result in an array of acts such as dressing in a way that is displeasing to parents, socializing with peers that the parents disapprove of, coming home past the set curfew time, and the list goes on. These aforementioned acts are not necessarily delinquent or harmful to the teenager but are often perceived that way by the parent. In turn, the parent may react negatively, leading the teenager to take further steps away from the parents' wishes.

The act of rebelling during the teenage years can take many different forms, and the results of teenage rebellion are not always what we as parents and educators may have in mind. Oftentimes, the image that first comes to mind is adolescents rebelling in order to engage in delinquent behaviors. That form of rebellion is only a small percentage of the acts of rebellion taking place in the teenage years. The truth is much of the rebellion that is acted out is non-delinquent and within the range of what is considered normal and healthy for adolescent development.

CHAPTER 6

Impact of Teenage Rebellion on Parents and Teachers

Sometimes parents feel that it is easier to give in than to argue. They become more permissive, to avoid the unpleasantness of a confrontation with a "sullen, withdrawn, and uncommunicative adolescent," and thus the child never learns to take a stand or make a decision. Permissiveness often results in loss of self-confidence on the part of the child. If parents do not support the child's decision to try new things, the child will feel they cannot try anything. Failure at any task may mean the adolescent will never attempt that task again. Though rebellion may be a positive act for the teenager, the parents often react in a negative way. This reaction causes added problems to the parent-child relationship and often on the child's self-esteem. The increase in problems at school and negative altercations with teachers is also a negative by-product of rebellion. There are often suspensions from school resulting from fights started by the adolescent or refusal to adhere to school rules. In subcultures where there is a high value placed on education, such as the Asian or Jewish-American culture, it is often the teachers who are the target of rebellion acts and who react most negatively. This can be frustrating for the teacher since they are used to success in dealing with children in earlier life stages.

CHAPTER 7

Effective Communication Strategies

B. Reflective Listening - This method involves listening to your teenager and then when you respond to what your teenager said, you restate in different words the meaning that your teenager was trying to communicate. This helps your teenager feel understood. An example of this would be if your teenager says "I can't stand it when my friends make plans with me and then cancel at the last minute. They don't even understand how that makes me feel." An effective reflective listening response would be "You feel really frustrated when your friends cancel plans they made with you because you think it's inconsiderate and takes you for granted." This will prompt your teenager to confirm that what you interpreted is what he or she actually meant or to correct you if you misunderstood. If you correctly understand your teenager, it will make your teenager feel understood and validated, and it will strengthen your rapport with your teenager.

1. Use "I" Statements - An "I" statement is a style of communication that focuses on the feelings or beliefs of the speaker rather than thoughts and characteristics that the speaker attributes to the listener. The method is to put the speaker's feelings forth in a manner that does not judge the listener, but only communicates

the feelings or beliefs in the situation that caused the feelings. This method is especially useful in tense situations or conflicts with your teenager because it reduces the likelihood that your teenager will feel attacked and be defensive in response. For instance, compare the difference between "You never make time to be with me doing something I want to do" to "I feel sad when I don't get to spend time with you".

Effective communication can make a tremendous difference not only in our ability to understand our teenagers' behaviors, but also in helping our teenagers feel understood. Below is a list of effective communication strategies to employ when dealing with your teenager. Remember that changing your communication style is not achieved overnight. It requires practice, patience, determination, and a willingness to change.

CHAPTER 8

Setting Boundaries and Consequences

The most important aspect of setting boundaries and consequences is that you are consistent and follow through every time the rule is broken. Reflect on the rule and make sure that the consequence you have set is fair, then communicate with your teen. Let her know that you love her, will support her, and that you will do your best to help her remember the rules you have set. She may be upset with you at first, but it is the consistent follow-through rather than the anger or the initial consequence that will lead to a change in behavior.

Decide which rules are most important to you in terms of safety and morality, and focus on these. Consequences should be set that teach the lessons you want your teen to learn. For instance, if you feel that it is very important for your teen to learn to take care of her possessions, a logical consequence if she is continually careless with them might be that you do not replace a possession that is carelessly lost or damaged. Other consequences for safety violations or things that are non-negotiable might include loss of driving or phone privileges.

CHAPTER 9

Building Trust and Empathy

The cornerstone for any kind of positive relationship with adolescents is the establishment of clarity, trust, and empathy. Essentially, the predictable presence of parents (or teachers) combined with predictability within limits can provide the structure that gives adolescents a sense of security. On a daily basis, this involves even-handed control, respectful communication, and the willingness to negotiate around family rules and their enforcement. Even-handed control refers to the consistent application of consequences (both positive and negative) in response to behavior, as well as the monitoring of undesirable behavior. Ideally, this should be combined with the provision of reasons for the control measures and the encouragement of adolescent questioning. When discipline leads to more open negotiation, it is all the more effective in promoting adolescent autonomy. Inevitably, trust and empathy are built through positive time spent together and an understanding of the adolescent's world. What adults may perceive as quality time (planned activities and outings) is not necessarily what adolescents define as positive time spent with them. Often, the most fruitful interactions come from spending informal time in the same vicinity as adolescents, which provides them with an easy opportunity for discussion as well as playing or simply being silly. United participation in hobbies or work that adolescents enjoy is another way of fostering open communication and showing involvement in their world, while rational discussion may be facilitated by an adult's attempt to learn something about teen culture (favorite music, latest fashion) and then ask the adolescent for their perspective on the matter. Furthermore, nothing screams mistrust than an adult snooping through an adolescent's belongings or personal space. Thus, it is crucial to respect their privacy unless there are serious concerns for their safety. Finally, learning to be empathetic involves active listening, efforts to understand situations from the adolescent's viewpoint, and consideration of their feelings when making decisions that affect them. An example from this author's personal experience was when his father wanted to use the family's dishwashing allowance as a means of teaching the financial concept that time equals money. After listening to the strong objections from the author and his sister and taking into account that they considered it unfair to miss out on other paying jobs in order to do unpaid work, their father changed his decision on the matter. He had still managed to negotiate a deal where the author and his sister would wash a set number of dishes in exchange for the money they would have received for the entire allowance and deemed this to be more fair and appropriate to the feelings of his children.

CHAPTER 10

Encouraging Independence and Decision-Making

Give your teenager a chance to make decisions about things that affect them. If you have always controlled the decisions, you might want to step back and think about what is actually reasonable for your teen to decide by themselves. Obviously, you will still need to set the rules about things that are non-negotiable, but choices about simple things like what to have for dinner, what to wear, and what time to go to bed will give your teenager a feeling of control and increase their confidence in decision making. If they are hesitant, help by listing the options with them and talking about the possible outcomes of each decision.

Support teenagers' efforts to make decisions. Encourage them to think about consequences and alternative actions. For example, sit down with your teenager and help them come up with options to a problem. Discuss with your teenager how they can identify the pros and cons of each option. Assist them in thinking about what decision is in their best interest and help them consider how this might affect the long term. By giving them your own opinion, telling them what you would do in that situation and why, don't be dismayed if your teenager chooses a different option. It's important for them to make their own decisions and learn from any mistakes that follow. Be there to help them if the consequences are too harsh.

CHAPTER 11

Managing Conflict and Anger

Managing conflict and anger is an essential skill in both personal and professional relationships. Conflict is a natural part of human interaction, and learning how to effectively manage it can lead to healthier and more productive relationships. When conflicts arise, it is important to address them in a calm and respectful manner. This involves active listening, expressing your thoughts and feelings clearly, and seeking to understand the other person's perspective. It is also important to avoid personal attacks and instead focus on the issue at hand. Anger is a normal emotion, but it is important to manage it in a healthy way. This can involve taking a step back and giving yourself time to cool down before addressing the situation. It is also helpful to identify the underlying causes of your anger and find constructive ways to address them. Overall, managing conflict and anger requires effective communication, empathy, and a willingness to find mutually beneficial solutions. By developing these skills, you can navigate conflicts more effectively and build stronger relationships.

CHAPTER 12

Supporting Mental and Emotional Well-being

It is important for teens to discuss and express how they feel and what they are thinking. Often they become accustomed to internalizing emotional problems and may not express the negative thoughts and feelings. If symptoms of depression arise, it is important to seek professional help. Cognitive behavior therapy has proven to be an effective form of treatment with teenage depression.

For example, after being told off by a teacher, a teenager may think they are always in trouble and that teachers hate them, when in reality they have a good relationship with many teachers and have a clean record. The degree of emotional response which stemmed from the event is also an important factor in identifying irrational thinking. If an incident has caused highly emotional upset which is prolonged and unrealistic, then it is likely that there is an irrational pattern of thinking involved. Encouraging the teen to change the negative thoughts and replace them with more balanced thinking is an important step in altering the way they feel.

It is important to identify and modify unhelpful or irrational negative thinking. There are two typical forms of this thinking: over-generalizing situations, taking one bad incident as a never-ending pattern of defeat;

and "all or nothing thinking," seeing things as black or white, bad or good, with nothing in between.

CHAPTER 13

Recognizing and Addressing Substance Abuse

Adolescence is a time in which young adults are trying to gain control over their lives, and often they do not make the best decisions. Experimentation is the mixing of different kinds of drugs or using drugs for other than their intended purpose (i.e., prescription medication), and it often leads to regular use. Abuse is that regular use which has negative consequences, and dependence is the compulsive use of a substance despite experiencing problems resulting from its use. It is important to distinguish abuse from dependence because adolescents who are dependent probably require some form of counseling or treatment to help them stop using, whereas an abuser can usually be helped to change his/her behavior with a brief intervention.

The use of drugs, alcohol, and tobacco is potentially detrimental to the emotional and physical development of adolescents and may also hinder their educational success. Most of these problems develop during the turbulent period of adolescence, although it must be noted that substance abuse is highly variable and not all youth who experiment with drugs develop a problem.

CHAPTER 14

Seeking Professional Help

Working with a professional If treatment recommendations are forthcoming, asking for an explanation of the rationale behind them, the therapeutic mechanisms involved, and the expected course and outcome of the proposed treatment can give a clearer understanding of what is being recommended and whether it is likely to help. At the same time, you may need to explain the cultural and personal meaning of seeking help and the problems at hand to the professional, since many mental health professionals have little understanding of or experience with normal adolescent rebellion and family dynamics, and many have only slight familiarity or only textbook familiarity with the common adolescent problems, misbehaviors, and emotions that lead parents to seek help.

First steps In many cultures, a family seeking professional help indicates a serious loss of face or a crisis situation. In Western society, many people only seek help when a problem has reached crisis proportions. Raising the subject of seeking outside help often will make teens and families uncomfortable. You may encounter significant resistance and some negotiations may be necessary. However, finding a mental health professional who can evaluate your teen and recommend a course of action may be helpful. Primary care physicians can also be a starting point for evaluation and referral. Understanding the professional standards of being warm, empathic, and nonjudgmental, a skilled professional should be able to develop a trusting relationship with your teen and engage him in treatment, as well as working with you to develop an understanding of your teen and a plan of action. Treatment recommendations may include individual or group therapy for the teen, family therapy, parent guidance, or psychopharmacology for certain conditions. A professional who is able to take decisive action and get family members engaged in treatment is likely to be more effective than one whose style is indirect and passive.

CHAPTER 15

Dealing with Peer Influence

Stay actively involved in your teen's life. Ask your teen about his/her friends, activities, and values. Expressing interest will show your teen that you care and are paying attention. Keeping the lines of communication open will encourage your teen to make better choices, and should it become apparent that your teen is engaging in high-risk behaviors, addressing the problem early will make it easier to find a solution. Be sure to have a realistic discussion with your teen about the effects of alcohol, drugs, and sexual activity. Scare tactics and exaggerations are not very effective and will cause your teen to lose trust in you should he/she be exposed to these situations and find them not to be as you described. Instead, try using facts and clear expectations to get your point across. Let your teen know that it is okay to refuse an offer to participate in high-risk behaviors, and he/she should have a plan for how to remove themselves from a negative situation. Brainstorm with your teen as to how he/she can resist negative peer pressure and make a list of some alternative activities to do with friends. Consider role-playing to allow your teen to practice refusal and resistance strategies. This will build confidence, and having a plan will make it easier for your teen to avoid the situation without feeling embarrassed. Help your teen find friends that share his/her values and interests. This may require involvement in community or extracurricular activities. Encourage healthy friendships by getting to know your teen's friends and welcoming them into your home. An accepting and understanding attitude will show your teen that he/she does not need to seek acceptance elsewhere.

Most parents and teachers are aware of how powerful peer pressure can be in influencing teen behavior. Teens may encounter increased pressure to engage in riskier behaviors and make poor choices when it comes to drugs, alcohol, and sexual activity. These behaviors can result from a variety of factors, such as media influence, curiosity, and boredom, low self-esteem, or attempting to appear grown-up. Although some degree of experimentation is normal during the teen years, it is important to help your teen understand that the long-term consequences of these behaviors may not be worth the short-term "benefits."

CHAPTER 16

Addressing Academic Challenges

* Research shows that the number of students who leave school during their teenage years because of academic challenges is relatively small. However, for many parents and teachers, the specter of failure and an empty future is the driving force behind their worries about rebellion. * When parents or teachers are dealing with a young person who is not achieving at school, it is important that they take a step back and look at the bigger picture. Firstly, they need to ascertain whether the child is having problems with a particular subject, with the school in general, or with education as a whole. It is not unusual for it to be the school or the particular teaching style or teachers that are causing the problem rather than the child's attitude to learning. If the child has negative feelings about the school, this can spill over to a more general negative attitude to learning. * When the problem appears to be subject-specific, the next step is to look at the child's feelings about the subject and find out the reasons for the negativity. In most cases, a child who is struggling with a particular subject will feel bad about themselves in relation to that subject. Low motivation and low self-esteem will result in avoidance of the subject both in and out of school. * Once the issues are clearer, specific plans can be made. A common mistake is for parents to try and solve the problem on behalf of the child by instructing them on

what to do. This may result in short-term improvement, but is unlikely to promote long-term development of the child. For issues of school or education in general, it will be negotiation with the child to identify what needs to change and how it might be changed. Temporarily letting go and allowing the child to experience the consequences of their own actions may be a hard thing to do, but it is often a necessary part of the learning process.

CHAPTER 17

Promoting Healthy Relationships

A healthy relationship is based upon equality and difference. No two people are the same, although you may have things in common. Both partners should express their opinions, feelings, and needs. Although they may not be the same, it is still important for both people's voices to be heard. Behaviors that promote equality in a relationship may include the following: listening to the other person non-judgmentally, being emotionally supportive, sharing decision-making, and taking responsibility for their partner when they are "not feeling up to par." A relationship of this nature should make both people feel good, emotionally comfortable, and open around each other. Anybody could be in a healthy relationship. It doesn't matter what age, race, gender, or sexuality you may be. Unfortunately, many relationships consist of people who do not treat each other equally. This could be due to characteristics of the relationship itself or the people involved in the relationship. Characteristics of an unhealthy relationship may include a cycle of fighting and making up over and over again, fearing your partner, having to change who you are to fit your partner's standards, and attempting to control your partner. These unhealthy relationships can take a toll on a person both mentally and physically. Whether the toll is taken immediately or it happens over time, these kinds of relationships could potentially change a person forever. A quick and effective way to evaluate your relationship is by taking the Equality Wheel assessment. This test will help you determine how equal and healthy your relationship is.

CHAPTER 18

Fostering Resilience and Self-Esteem

So the question is, how can these characteristics be built and fostered in our teens? Whether a teen has low self-esteem and poor resilience, or they are just too passive in dealing with situations, help and guidance from parents and adults is crucial.

Resilience is the ability to bounce back from a difficult situation or crisis. An individual with high resilience will maintain a stable frame of mind during a crisis, think of solutions, and take actions to resolve the crisis, ultimately resulting in the crisis having a positive resolution. These are key characteristics that you should want to instill in your teen as they will be able to handle difficult life situations in a healthy, positive way. This is so crucial as through the teen years, from moving from city to city and changing schools, to relationships with parents and peers, teens will certainly encounter many difficult and trying situations. They need these traits to get them through these situations, which will ultimately help to shape who they become as adults.

Self-esteem is an overall feeling of self-worth and the belief in one's abilities. It is an important factor as high self-esteem can reduce the chances of a teen experiencing depression and other psychological disorders. Teens with high self-esteem are also more likely to make healthy decisions, while those with low self-esteem are more likely to give in to negative peer pressure and make poor choices. Teens with high self-esteem are also more likely to have the ability to handle difficult situations, such as the divorce of their parents, and come out with a more healthy resolution.

CHAPTER 19

Understanding Cultural and Gender Factors

The transition from childhood to adolescence differs in many respects for boys and girls. However, there are also individual differences in this regard that are equally as important. As we attempt to understand individual teenagers, the first relevant issue is the way in which they regard their own selves and how they believe that others perceive them. These self-perceptions and the importance attached to them vary in different societies. An adolescent girl in a traditional society may regard herself, and be regarded by others, as a woman. In such cultures, the onset of adolescence for girls is marked by social and religious rites of passage. In societies such as the USA, emphasis is placed largely upon individual roles, as opposed to fixed roles determined by age, and adolescents may strive to distance themselves from adults in certain respects while at the same time emulating them in other respects. How adolescents view themselves and others view them is vitally important in understanding their behavior. For example, a teenager who comes from an ethnic minority and lives in a country in which ethnicity is a means of distinguishing status and entitlement will have different behaviors and academic expectations compared to a teenager from the majority culture.

CHAPTER 20

Balancing Freedom and Responsibility

While giving teens independence, providing opportunities for leadership and autonomous decision making, and developing their individuality, you still need to enforce some boundaries to ensure their safety. Allowing too much freedom can be just as dangerous as not allowing enough. This is a difficult balancing act for parents, and often involves a great deal of trial and error. You are not alone if you sometimes feel unsure as to when to maintain your ground and when to let go. Set clear limits that are to be enforced no matter what, and allow freedom in other areas which can be negotiated if they encroach on the non-negotiable limits. For example, curfew times may be non-negotiable but the time to be home for dinner could be negotiated. When negotiating limits, it's a good idea to allow older teens more leeway and say in making the rules that affect them. They will be much more likely to comply with limits which they have set for themselves. Always ensure that the consequences of their actions are reasonable and fully explained. A punishment that far exceeds the offense is likely to cause resentment and will not be effective in teaching responsibility.

CHAPTER 21

Strategies for Teachers in the Classroom

When addressing negative behavior, it is extremely important that a teacher criticizes the act and not the student. Often times teens develop a false image of themselves as being bad people because of the problems they have attributed on their behavior. A teacher should explain how the problem behavior has negative effects, and present solutions to the problem. Teachers should also avoid power struggles with problem students. This only further encourages the student's defiance. As a sign of good will, a teacher can make offers for special privileges or rewards for a student making changes in their behavior. This is not to be mistaken in bribing the student, rather it is positive reinforcement, for change of negative behavior.

First and foremost, a teacher must set very clear and concrete expectations. Teens do not want to have to guess what is expected of them, and will be less likely to revolt against something that they knew in the first place. Because often time teachers are dealing with a rebellious teen student of whom their problem behavior is a cry for help, teachers should stress a concern for the students well-being. They should openly recognize their concern for the student when they know the student is capable of doing better, and tell them that they will not accept such behavior, because they know that they are a better person, and can improve. This is a good segue into directly addressing the problem behavior.

A teenager's life revolves around the classroom, whether they admit it or not. How they perform in school is a very realistic gauge of how their rebellion is affecting their life. A teacher is in a position of power in a teen's life, as much as they do not want to admit it. Teachers are authority figures, and often times are involved in a mini-power struggle with a rebellious student. Teachers do not have to stand and take the negative attitude that a rebellious teen dishes out. There are several strategies that teachers can take in the classroom in order to make it a more comfortable environment for a rebellious teen.

CHAPTER 22

Collaborating with Parents and Guardians

The goal of any communication with the parent is to maintain a professional relationship in which the teacher conveys concern for the student and seeks input from the parent on how to best handle the student's behavior.

To keep an open line of communication, many schools are requiring teachers to post office hours for phone calls to parents, while others are giving teachers time during the day to make phone calls using student information that is provided by the parents. Email has also become an effective tool for communication that can be utilized with the increasing availability of the internet to teachers and parents. A monthly progress report can also be requested by the parent to keep them informed on the student's behavior. This availability of information is important so that parents do not have to rely on second hand or incomplete information from the student.

It is imperative that effective communication is established between the school and the parent when working with the rebellious student. Each party has information that is vital to the success of the intervention. Teachers may be informed of an event in the student's life that is directly related to their behavior in the school. Likewise, the parent may have noticed a change in behavior at home but is unaware of the events that have taken place in school. Regular communication can keep both parties informed and take into account the entire scope of the student's behavior. Open dialogue can also prevent the "blame game" where a teacher blames the student for behavior in school and the parent blames the teacher for problems at home.

CHAPTER 23

Creating a Supportive School Environment

Timing and coordination of program implementation in a school is another key consideration. Students transferring from another school may be exposed to a new program and a different method of discipline. This presents a risk to the experimental group in terms of deviant peer avoidance and contact with the comparison group. If the comparison group is exposed to the new method or program, this could contaminate the study and program effects may not be directly attributable. For these reasons, a level of flexibility, which should be specified in a study protocol, regarding the order in which schools take on these programs is necessary. This may involve delayed recruitment of the experimental group in schools in which program implementation is scheduled for a later date.

Studies of various programs have highlighted the importance of access to caring adults - through both positive student-teacher relationships and access to counselors - on student outcomes. Programs targeting youth at risk of delinquency have been found to be most effective in environments with a high level of teacher support and implementation of clear behavior and academic expectations. The best way to ensure student safety and promote positive adult-to-student interactions may be placement in smaller schools or schools within schools, so long as this does not mean isolation from all but deviant peers.

The school environment can play a key role in determining the success of a program aimed at intervening in the lives of troubled students. Preliminary research on alternative education and the effects of small class size in regular schools on student outcomes indicates that schools seeking to implement programs directed toward difficult students will be most effective in facilities that offer a safe and supportive environment. Random assignment studies have demonstrated the potential harm of placement among deviant peers on those already predisposed to delinquency. Only in supportive environments have such interventions been found effective. Thus, it is essential to make the safety and welfare of the students participating in these programs a top priority.

CHAPTER 24

Identifying Warning Signs
of Serious Issues

1. Prolonged negative mood, often accompanied by poor performance in school, withdrawal from extracurricular activities, and sometimes issues of running away from home. 2. Intense feelings of irritability or anger, usually indicated by frequent displays of aggressive behavior, often getting into fights and confrontations. 3. Dramatic changes in behavior, such as sudden refusal to communicate, paranoia, peculiar thoughts or beliefs, expressing overwhelming guilt, or prolonged anxiety. 4. Changes in eating or sleeping patterns, often leading to significant weight loss or gain. 5. Extreme difficulty in adapting to situations, whether it be at home, at school with friends, or with life circumstances. 6. Acts of harming oneself or mentioning thoughts to do so.

Changes in your child's behavior can be a mystery. It may be hard to tell whether or not they are just going through some of the typical, normal teenage angst or if their behavior is indicating something more serious. With statistics stating that in 2011, an alarming 20% of Canadian post-secondary students reported having thought about suicide, and that the rate of hospitalization for youth with mental health issues has increased by 66% in the last 10 years, knowing how to spot the difference has become crucial for parents and teachers. Here are some warning signs that indicate more serious issues may be at hand:

CHAPTER 25

Interventions for High-Risk Behaviors

Also, consider the following options for evaluating the necessity of different strategies for parental involvement recommended by Jon Bishop and Suzie Wignall: - Confrontational interventions, where parents share information they have discovered about their child's risky behavior and demand an explanation. - Discussion and negotiated punishment, where the teenager and parent weigh the pros and cons of stopping the behavior and come to an agreement on the level of punishment or restrictions, should the behavior continue. This approach presupposes that the teenager is not fully committed to the behavior and is willing to consider change.

High-risk behaviors present complex and thorny problems with no easy solutions. The primary dilemma surrounds issues of privacy and choice. Many high-risk behaviors, such as drug use and sexual activity, are kept secret in order to avoid adults' helpful interventions. Discussing this issue with our teenagers can be helpful, as it opens the door for clear negotiation of when parental involvement may or may not be appropriate. Generally speaking, parental involvement should be higher when: - The behavior in question is particularly dangerous. - Intervention can occur at an early stage of the behavior, preventing more serious involvement. - The adolescent is struggling with personal conflict about involvement in the behavior.

CHAPTER 26

Resolving Conflict between Parents and Teachers

Teachers and parents may not always agree, but when they come together and act as good role models, the child has the best chances for success. There are a number of positive ways to bring together parents and teachers. If the parent-teacher conference becomes a blaming session, both the teacher and the parent may feel attacked and become defensive. In these situations, very little is accomplished in the way of helping the student. Instead, plan the conference and put things in a more positive perspective so that everyone is a part of the solution. Teachers and parents can also check with guidance counselors, who often have good insights and are able to mediate between the two parties effectively. A solution that often has children on their best behavior is having them sit in on the parent-teacher conference. This puts extra pressure on the child to follow through in a desired way, making it a win-win situation for both the teachers and parents. With highly involved parents, teacher-parent disagreements may show the student that he or she can manipulate situations his or her way. In these cases, parents can examine their own attitudes and actions to see if they are contributing to the teacher's perception of them. Remember, it is easier to change your child than to change the teacher. If the teacher is committed to the child, parents should make an effort to understand the teacher's needs/reservations and accommodate where possible. By being flexible and compromising with the teacher, the parent shows the child that the teacher is a respected authority figure, and that he or she will be held accountable.

CHAPTER 27

Promoting Positive Parent-Teen Relationships

Studies show that a strong relationship with both parents, whether they're together or not, helps teens to feel loved and secure. With this foundation, teens are more likely to make better decisions and exhibit less delinquent behavior. Although teenagers may rebel against this idea, they really need ongoing supervision, monitoring, and positive role models to make it safely through the adolescent years. And they need parents who are united in the effort to rear them.

Teenagers need parents to be warm and affectionate with them. They also need the consistent, ongoing presence and interest of both parents in their lives. So even if a parent and teen are living apart in a situation of joint custody, it is imperative that both parents are equally involved in parenting. This means sharing the rights and responsibilities of decision-making, recognizing the importance of continuing contact with the teen, and allowing the teen equal access to both parents.

A strong and positive parent-teen relationship can prevent delinquent behavior in diverse families, including those with step-parents and single parents. High levels of family bonding and low levels of conflict in the parent-teen relationship have been shown to be associated with less involvement in delinquent acts in a study of middle and high school students.

A study of 14-15 year-olds whose parents were going through a divorce found that these teens were more likely to participate in delinquent acts. They felt as though they were not attached to their parents and hence did not need to abide by the rules.

Studies show that children, including teenagers, who are not disciplined and who do not receive affection and moral support from their parents, may be drawn to negative influences. Indeed, without positive parental support, teenagers may be lured by delinquent behavior.

Showing affection to teens, including hugging, a pat on the back, or an arm around the shoulder, is a step towards positive, supportive relationships. For some parents, it is second nature to show our love physically. But for others, it doesn't come naturally. They don't even think about how to show warmth to their children.

CHAPTER 28

Addressing Rebellion in Different Developmental Stages

Understanding the developmental stage of the adolescent and their reasons for rebelling are important when considering how to approach and intervene with the rebellious behavior.

At later developmental stages, rebellious behavior can be a result of a teenager feeling that they have not or cannot reach the expectations of their parents. This can be regarding any number of achievements, including school performance, sporting achievements, or goals which the parents had for the teenager. If a child feels that they have failed or not succeeded in what their parents expected of them, they may exhibit self-destructive behaviors and refusal to comply by order of their parents.

The strength of this relationship is evident in early to mid-adolescence when the teenager is deciding about their long-term goals and aspirations in terms of their future career and family plans. It is at this time that if the adolescent has a trusting relationship and open communication with their parents, they are likely to adopt their parents' values when deciding what they want to do with their life. This is a critical point, as if the teenager has not adopted their parents' values or does not have a trusting relationship with their parents, it is likely they will make a decision which is contrary to their parents' desires, and rebellious behavior may result if the parents attempt to dissuade them.

Adolescents at different developmental stages exhibit different strengths and capabilities, which are essential when assessing how to approach and intervene when a teenager displays rebellious behavior. Children are in need of protection, guidance, and direction from their parents, and if this is achieved, a trusting attachment is formed. If a trusting relationship is maintained between parent and child, the child will adopt the values and belief system of his/her parents.

CHAPTER 29

Supporting LGBTQ+ Adolescents

- Learn more about LGBTQ+ issues (and encourage their child to share information) - Take a clear stand against discrimination and harassment of LGBTQ+ individuals - Show unwavering support and love for their child

Studies have consistently shown that parental support is crucial to the well-being and healthy development of youth. Adolescents whose parents are involved in their lives in a positive way are happier, healthier, and do better in school. This is also the case for LGBTQ+ young people; however, they may need extra support during this time. Parents can be supportive of their LGBTQ+ young person by taking the following steps:

It is not uncommon for parents to have difficulty when they first learn that their child is LGBTQ+. People have many different understandings of and attitudes about sexual orientation. Because of this diversity in attitudes, as well as the widespread silence about sexual orientation, parents often have little accurate information about LGBTQ+ issues. Some parents may also feel that they will be stigmatized by others if their child is LGBTQ+. All of this can leave parents uncertain about how they can best support their child.

Parents of LGBTQ+ Adolescents

Adolescence can be especially challenging for young people who are LGBTQ+. It can be a time of both self-discovery and uncertainty. Having supportive and accepting parents and school staff can be very helpful for these young people as they navigate through this time. Parents and schools can better support LGBTQ+ youth by creating an environment that is accepting and by being an ally to these young people.

Supporting LGBTQ+ Adolescents

CHAPTER 30

Addressing Technology and Social Media Influence

On a positive note, technology and social media create new opportunities for parents to connect with their teenagers. Though they can seem secretive, teenagers often desire greater parent involvement in their lives. A study conducted by the Pew Internet & American Life Project found that 83% of teenagers aged 12-17 do not feel that their parents regularly interfere with their internet use. Yet, many teenagers desire adult guidance on how to use the internet, information, and tools to improve their lives. Compared with offline parents, digital teenagers are more excited about discussing and receiving advice on adolescent internet use. Eager for more parental guidance, many teenagers think that their parents were doing a good job of preparing them for the real world where tough situations can arise online.

This 'cyberbullying' presents an ongoing torment for victims as there is no escape or safe place. The potential for hundreds of peers to witness or participate in online bullying incidents can amplify the severity of the victims' experience. The hostile, invasive, and public nature of cyberbullying is often more emotionally damaging for victims than traditional bullying. Another negative byproduct of increased technology use is the rise in sedentary lifestyles and obesity in teenagers. With global usage, teens spend more time indoors, often alone and sitting, while engaged with technology. Social media can also have negative effects on teenagers' body image and mental health. These influences can create great concern for parents.

Interchanging technological and societal influences create a new and challenging environment for parent/teenager relationships. The access to technology has rendered teenagers absorbed in virtual worlds rather than the real one. At the same time, technology use can connect people in ways never before possible. Social media sites such as Facebook and Twitter give teenagers new platforms for interacting with friends and expressing themselves. Parents need to understand how the internet and mobile devices are changing their children's social lives. Technology and social media can present both positive and negative influences for teenagers. New technology has created new possibilities for bullying to occur, be it through anonymous emails, texts, or spreading rumors online.

Figure 30

CHAPTER 31

Encouraging Healthy Hobbies and Activities

Encouraging your child to do something that broadens their abilities is giving them a huge advantage for their future. Hobbies provide positive challenges that are fun to do. Encouraging your child to engage in hobbies that develop healthy skills is a core part of positive parenting. A healthy hobby would be one that channels a child's energy into an activity, which is beneficial on a number of levels. This will reduce the probability of the child finding unhealthy alternatives to spend their time. Making models, crafting, playing musical instruments, gardening, and cooking are all examples of hobbies. These activities can be done alone or in a group, and can be a casual or organized pursuit. The key is that it is an activity that is personally set out to achieve an enjoyable result. This will provide the child with a sense of achievement and increased self-esteem when skills improve and projects are completed. Spending time helping your child to learn the skills involved in their hobby will increase your bonding and provide a positive and rewarding experience for both parties. This positive interaction will provide a valuable alternative to methods of discipline and encourage the child to remain committed to their hobby. Sports and physical activities are also extremely valuable to a growing child. A team sport significantly helps in the development of social skills. Learning to communicate, take turns, and work as part of a team are all vital skills in the child's future. Any physical activity is a great form of stress relief and it keeps the body healthy. Try to avoid using physical activity as punishment, as this will create negative connotations with effort and the activity itself.

CHAPTER 32

Conclusion and Final Thoughts

It should be clear from this paper that the journey through adolescence is not simple and is often tumultuous. Therefore, it is important that we don't give up on young people, even if they exhibit problem behaviors, and that we maintain a compassionate stance toward the issues that they must confront. By better understanding the difficulties that adolescents face and being patient, supportive, and providing them with the opportunities they need, parents and others involved with young people can help guide them through these difficult times. At times, parents may feel that they are ineffectual in protecting youth from some of the pitfalls that have been described in this paper. It is important that they don't despair in instances when things have not gone well, as it is never too late to provide young people with the support that they need.

In providing a guide on how to parent, one should be wary of giving advice that is overly prescriptive, as what is appropriate will depend on many factors. Instead, we provide the developmental information needed to make informed decisions as to what will help adolescents best negotiate the specific challenges that they will face.

The transition to adolescence is a time of rapid change for children and their parents. While the child's journey through adolescence is not easy, parenting through the teenage years also poses new challenges.

This paper provides a framework for understanding the transition of adolescents from the broader cultural context and makes some suggestions as to what can be done to improve our society's treatment of young people. At its core is the argument that the developmental needs of young people are often not well served by many of the institutions they find themselves in and around. Nowhere is this more apparent than with the issue of juvenile offending. The treatment of adolescents when they come into conflict with the law is addressed. Another realm in which adults often fail young people is in recognizing and supporting their developing capacities. This is often difficult as it necessitates a shift in the balance of power between adults and youth, but it is essential in order for young people to reach their adult potential, and a failure to do so can have dire consequences for society in the future.

9 798869 371867